State Your Case

Evaluating Arguments About
Education

James Bow

CRABTREE
PUBLISHING COMPANY
WWW.CRABTREEBOOKS.COM

D1361451

Author: James Bow

Series research and development: Reagan Miller

Editors: Sarah Eason, Claudia Martin,
  Jennifer Sanderson, and Janine Deschenes

Proofreaders: Tracey Kelly, Wendy Scavuzzo

Indexer: Tracey Kelly

Editorial director: Kathy Middleton

Design: Paul Myerscough and Steve Mead

Cover design: Katherine Berti

Photo research: Claudia Martin

**Production coordinator and
  Prepress technician:** Katherine Berti

Print coordinator: Katherine Berti

Produced for Crabtree Publishing Company
by Calcium Creative Ltd

Photo Credits:
t=Top, c=Center, b=Bottom, l=Left, r=Right.

Inside: Shutterstock: Andrey_Popov: p.34; antoniodiaz: p.7; Antonio
Guillem: p.39; AVAVA: p.32; Chaay Tee: p.27; Denis Kuvaev: p.41;
DGLimages: p.36; forestpath: p.25; Goodluz: p.19; Iakov Filimonov:
p.31; Jacob Lund: pp.1, 17; Joshua Resnick: p.28; Kamira: p.29; Kent
Hilbert: p.4; LightField Studios: p.22; LStockStudio: p.43; Marco
Saroldi: p.16; Michael Jung: pp.3, 8, 14; Monkey Business Images:
pp.6, 9, 13, 20, 30, 33, 35, 37, 38; Olesia Bilkei: p.40; Peter Snaterse:
p.12; Rawpixel.com: p.5; science photo: p.26; SpeedKingz: pp.21, 24;
Suwin: p.23; Syda Productions: p.18; Tom Wang: p.15; Travel Stock:
p.10; Vcoscaron: p.42; Vlad Karavaev: p.11.

Cover: Shutterstock: val lawless (r)
All other images from Shutterstock

Library and Archives Canada Cataloguing in Publication

Bow, James, 1972-, author
     Evaluating arguments about education / James Bow.

(State your case)
Includes bibliographical references and index.
Issued in print and electronic formats.
ISBN 978-0-7787-5076-5 (hardcover).--
ISBN 978-0-7787-5089-5 (softcover).--
ISBN 978-1-4271-2161-5 (HTML)

     1. Education--Juvenile literature. 2. Education--Philosophy—
Juvenileliterature. 3. Education--Aims and objectives--Juvenile
literature. 4. Education--Curricula--Juvenile literature. 5. Critical
thinking--Juvenile literature.6. Thought and thinking--Juvenile
literature. 7. Reasoning--Juvenile literature.8. Persuasion (Rhetoric)--
Juvenile literature. I. Title.

LB14.7.B695 2018   j370.1   C2018-903027-5
                                                         C2018-903028-3

Library of Congress Cataloging-in-Publication Data

CIP available at the Library of Congress

Crabtree Publishing Company
www.crabtreebooks.com   1-800-387-7650

Printed in the U.S.A./092018/CG20180810

Copyright © **2019 CRABTREE PUBLISHING COMPANY**. All rights reserved. No part of this publication may be reproduced, stored in a retrieval
system, or be transmitted in any form or by any means, electronic, mechanical, photocopying, recording, or otherwise, without the prior written
permission of Crabtree Publishing Company. In Canada: We acknowledge the financial support of the Government of Canada through the
Canada Book Fund for our publishing activities.

**Published in Canada
Crabtree Publishing**
616 Welland Ave.
St. Catharines, Ontario
L2M 5V6

**Published in the United States
Crabtree Publishing**
PMB 59051
350 Fifth Avenue, 59th Floor
New York, New York 10118

**Published in the United Kingdom
Crabtree Publishing**
Maritime House
Basin Road North, Hove
BN41 1WR

**Published in Australia
Crabtree Publishing**
3 Charles Street
Coburg North
VIC, 3058

CONTENTS

CHAPTER 1

EDUCATION TODAY AND TOMORROW

Knowledge is what separates us from other animals, and we gain knowledge through education. When we are born, we need constant care and attention. We are not born with the knowledge of how the seasons work, when we should plant crops, or how we can run machines or invent computers to make our lives easier. We all need education to succeed in our world.

A Key Part of Our Lives

We can learn new things throughout our lives, but children need to start learning early. We do most of our growing as children, and that includes brain development. As babies, we start to explore and learn about our environment. We learn to speak by listening to the people around us. We learn to walk and run through play. By the time we are five or six years old, we are ready to learn more complicated things, such as math and reading. That is when we go to school.

In the United States, the average student spends 1,016 hours per year in a school. Most **public education** systems expect students to stay in school for at least 12 years. Universities and colleges can add even more years to a person's education. There are also **apprenticeships** and **vocational** schools where students can study for a particular profession, such as electrician, mechanic, hairstylist, or chef.

In many places, children start school at age five, but some states are opening kindergartens and early education centers to children as young as three.

Educators are trying to teach students more about science, technology, engineering, and math (**STEM**). There are also many initiatives, or efforts, to get young women involved in STEM subjects.

Education is considered by many to be a **human right**. This is one reason why, in many countries, parents typically do not have to pay for their children to go to school. For example, in the United States and Canada, children's public education costs are paid for by **taxes**, and school is **compulsory**. Even if parents decide not to send their children to public schools, they are required to pay to send their children to private schools or educate their children themselves at home—and prove to the government that they are doing it.

Change in Our Future

Education has come a long way from the nineteenth century, when a single teacher often taught reading, writing, and **arithmetic** (a branch of math) to students of many different grades in a one-room schoolhouse. Although many schools still rely on teachers standing at the front of classrooms to teach children the skills required by the **curriculum**, today, changing technology has changed teaching methods.

Televisions and computers have given teachers and students access to educational programs to teach concepts in school and at home. Students can research topics using digital libraries and Internet resources. Digital programs and **simulators** can show students how the insides of animals work, how people lived in ancient cities, or how machines are built. Students who cannot go to school because they are unwell or live too far away can learn at home on computers. Students in classrooms around the world can connect with each other using video conferences. The curriculum has also changed dramatically over the years with science subjects such as computer coding and design; languages such as Mandarin and Japanese; and arts such as music production now taught in many schools with the help of technology.

Education: A Hot Topic

Our experiences at school shape who we become as adults, so a lot of people have strong opinions about many issues surrounding education. How many years should we go to school? Are tests and homework a good way to assess students' knowledge? Should teachers focus on math and science, or should they spend more time on languages, history, art, and music? Is it fair for teachers to assign extra homework?

As technology brings changes to education, more arguments are brewing. Are computers and tablets in the classroom helping children prepare for a future working with computers, or are they distracting students from their education? Now that we can access a world of information on the Internet, do we need school libraries anymore? Is there a benefit to learning completely online?

Arguing About Education

You may have heard many arguments that present people's opinions about these issues in education. People make arguments in the news, at school board meetings, and in principals' offices. With all of the arguments about education that you hear from day to day, you need to be able to work through the arguments to decide which ones are **credible**, and which are not. That way, you can start to form your own opinions about issues surrounding education, and how they affect you.

In this book, we will take a look at some arguments about education. We'll look at the features of an argument, what makes a strong argument, and how to decide whether you agree with it or not. Let's start by taking a look at the argument about **standardized** testing on the opposite page.

New technology is being brought into the classroom to help students learn. But is this technology always a good thing?

Do You Agree?

"Should all schools use standardized tests?"

STANDARDIZED TESTS ARE A GOOD MEASURE OF PROGRESS.

Since they compare students across schools, standardized tests are good tools to show how well schools are teaching students. Teachers can use test results to identify what areas students need more help in. Comparing students with one another also makes it easier to identify students with **learning disabilities**, so they can be given extra help.

Countries such as China and Japan, which are known for their high student achievement, use standardized tests. According to a report by the research firm McKinsey & Company, 20 school systems that brought in standardized tests "achieved significant, sustained, and widespread gains" in their students' education. Standardized tests are also popular with parents. According to a Center for Public Affairs Research survey, 75 percent of parents said these tests were "a solid measure of their children's abilities."

After reading the arguments about tests, decide which side you agree with. How did you make your choice? Did you rely on personal experience? Does the way the arguments are presented influence your decision?

STANDARDIZED TESTS ARE NOT A GOOD MEASURE OF PROGRESS.

In many cases, standardized tests measure only how well a student prepares for and performs during a test. Other issues that can affect student performance are not accounted for, such as stress, energy, and challenges such as learning disabilities. In some cases, a teacher's pay depends on how well their students perform on standardized tests. In others, students may be held back a grade by failing a test. For these reasons, teachers sometimes "teach to the test," which means that they teach students only to prepare for the test instead of addressing the needs of individual students.

A survey from the National Education Association found that 70 percent of teachers felt that standardized tests were not appropriate tools for measuring the performance of young students. Since 2002, when standardized tests were required in the United States, a **study** from the National Research Council showed no improvement in student achievement. The Center on Education Policy revealed that, since 2002, 44 percent of school districts reduced the time spent teaching arts, science, and social studies, and put more time into the test subjects of reading and math.

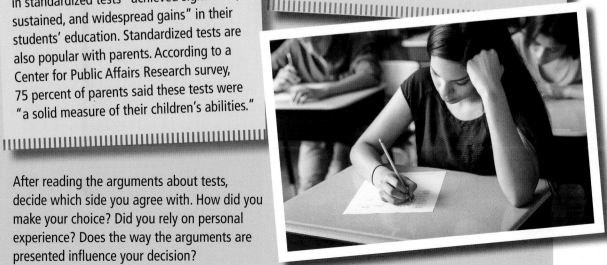

*When a person makes an argument about an issue that they feel strongly about, he or she will try to put forward their point of view clearly and **persuasively**.*

An argument is a set of reasons based on **logic** that shows a person's belief or position on an issue is **valid**, or correct. An argument can be used to try to change another person's point of view, or to persuade them to accept a new one. Arguments can also be used to draw support or promote action for a cause.

Why Argue?

You read, hear, and see arguments every day. You see people on the news, arguing that school days should start earlier or that schools should teach math and sciences more and physical education less. Each person states their ideas, gives their reasons, and if their argument is strong, supports their reasons with **evidence** to try to persuade others that their ideas are best.

Arguments are used in many different ways. Sometimes an argument can help people learn about an issue. It might explain one or both sides of an issue, so people can make an informed decision about what they believe. For example, it might explain that it is damaging, rather than helpful, to require a child to repeat a grade.

Other arguments are used to gather support for a cause, such as making it compulsory for children to start school a year earlier, at age four. This type of argument, called a persuasive argument, tries to get people to agree with that person's beliefs. It is meant to influence the way you think about something, or to change your mind about an issue.

Other arguments are used to solve problems and make decisions, such as whether or not students should be forced to take physical education courses every year. When both sides of an argument are heard, people can come to a decision about how they should act on an issue.

Arguments are not always serious. Sometimes people present arguments to learn about and discuss opposing ideas.

Prove Your Point

An argument is made up of a number of **claims**, or statements, about why a viewpoint is correct. To prove that your claims are valid, you need to give evidence that supports the things you say. Without this evidence, there is no way to prove that your claims are true. When you are **evaluating** an argument, it is up to you to decide whether the person making the argument has supported their claims with enough evidence.

Newspaper columnists often make arguments that express and defend their point of view about a current topic.

Building an Argument

A good argument needs to be carefully built. It has the following features, or parts:

Core Argument

The **core argument** is your position, or where you stand, on the topic or issue. Your core argument states what you believe to be true. It is the main point that you will try to prove in your argument. Arguments state the core argument in their introduction. An example of a core argument is:

> *Education should be compulsory for every child on Earth.*

> *According to **UNESCO**, in 40 out of 93 countries in the **developing world**, fewer than half of the poorest children finish primary school.*

Claims

Your claims are the statements that support your core argument. An example of a claim is:

> *Education is a human right because it is vital for people to be able to succeed in the world.*

Reasons

Reasons are details that support your claim. Reasons explain why you have made that specific claim. An example of a reason is:

> *People need education to gain the knowledge they need to find work and learn about their human rights.*

Evidence

A good argument supports its reasons with evidence. Evidence might be a quotation from an interview with someone who is considered to be an expert on the topic. It could be **statistics** from a study of people affected by an issue, or facts about the topic. Without evidence, an argument cannot be proven to be true.

Not everything you read is credible, so you need to assess if the evidence is valid. You can do this by asking questions such as:
- Who is the author of the source of information? Are they knowledgeable in the subject?
- Where did the information come from? Is it a respected organization?
- When was the source written? If it was several years ago, the information might be out of date.
- Do other sources have similar information? If not, you may need to evaluate whether the source is credible.

This is an example of credible evidence. It comes from a respected organization—the **United Nations**:

The United Nations Universal Declaration of Human Rights, a key document for the United Nations and the 193 countries that belong to it, lists education as a human right. Article 26 states, "Everyone has the right to education. Education shall be free, at least in the elementary and fundamental stages. Elementary education shall be compulsory."

Counterclaims

To make an argument even stronger, a person needs to take note of the possible **counterclaims** against their argument. Counterclaims are the claims that support the opposite viewpoint to the argument.

After making claims and giving reasons and evidence, a person making an argument should write down the strongest counterclaim against their argument. They should then respond to the counterclaim, using evidence, to prove why their argument is stronger. This is an example of a counterclaim:

There are people who say that forcing developing nations to educate all their children for free costs them too much, when they struggle to provide food and water for them. Access to clean water is a more important human right than education. According to the charity WaterAid, 844 million people do not have clean water, and as a result, every 2 minutes, a child under five dies from diarrhea. However, without education, people cannot learn about the health risks they face and how to improve them.

Conclusion

Your conclusion should restate your main argument and reasons. An example of a conclusion is:

Education helps everyone earn a living and care for themselves. Without education, people may not understand their human rights or recognize when they are being violated, or abused. To ensure a world where people are free and safe, everybody needs an education. That is why education is possibly the most important of all human rights.

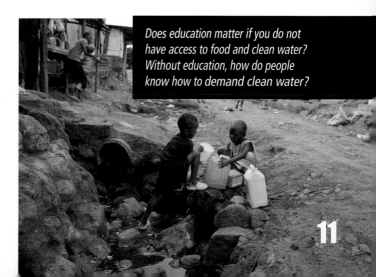

Does education matter if you do not have access to food and clean water? Without education, how do people know how to demand clean water?

11

Evaluating an Argument

You can evaluate an argument by looking at its features. Examine the argument below about whether high schools should begin their school days later in the morning. Does the argument include all of the features it needs to be a strong argument? When you have finished reading, decide if you think this argument is strong.

CORE ARGUMENT

High school days should start after 10 a.m., for the benefit of teenagers' learning and well-being.

CLAIM

Starting the high school day later would help teenagers perform better at school.

REASON

Teenagers need more sleep than adults. Their natural **sleep cycles** cause them to fall asleep later in the evenings and wake up later in the mornings. Forcing them to go to school early leaves them tired and less able to learn.

EVIDENCE

The American Academy of Sleep Medicine (AASM) recommends that teenagers get 8 to 10 hours of sleep each night. However, according to the Centers for Disease Control and Prevention (CDC), 70 percent of high school students sleep 7 hours or less per night. Researchers at McGill University found that it is more difficult for teenagers to fall asleep before 11 p.m., meaning that early school starts are preventing teenagers from getting a full night's sleep. A University of Minnesota study looked at 9,000 students at eight high schools. It found that those schools that moved their start times to later in the day allowed 60 percent of students to get 8 or more hours of sleep, boosted attendance, improved test scores in math, English, science, and social studies, and decreased the number of car crashes involving students by 70 percent.

*The body produces the hormone **melatonin** to help people sleep. According to an Oxford University study, some teenagers do not start producing melatonin until 1 a.m.*

Motor vehicle collisions are the leading cause of death for teenagers in the United States and Canada.

CLAIM

Keeping teenagers in school until later in the afternoon would reduce the number of car crashes involving teen drivers.

REASON

To drive a car safely, everyone needs to get enough sleep. If teenagers are regularly getting less than 8 hours sleep because of late nights and early school start times, they are likely to be more tired and distracted behind the wheel. This puts at risk not just their own lives, but the lives of their passengers, other road users, and pedestrians.

EVIDENCE

In Virginia, a 2011 study showed there were 65.8 crashes per 1,000 teen drivers in Virginia Beach compared to 46.6 crashes in neighboring Chesapeake. Virginia Beach students started high school at 7:20 a.m. In Chesapeak, they started at 8:40 a.m.

COUNTERCLAIM

Changing the times of the school day would be a big task. It would involve rearranging bus schedules, **extracurricular** activities, and teacher schedules, all of which would have a cost. However, reducing student car crashes would produce substantial savings to the health care system. Improving student achievement would mean students could grow up to work better jobs, earn higher wages, and pay more in taxes.

CONCLUSION

Given that teenagers' sleep cycles cause them to stay up later and sleep in later, and that students who get enough sleep perform better at school, moving high school to later in the day will help teenagers now and into the future. It is also essential that we reduce the numbers of teens killed and injured in car crashes.
Given these benefits, it is time to let teenagers sleep in.

Making a Great Argument

A core argument, claims, reasons, evidence, counterclaims, and conclusions are the important parts of an argument. But there are also other elements that make a great argument.

Who Is Your Audience?

Knowing who your **audience** is will help you target your argument. You can base your argument on details about your audience, such as its average age, **gender**, or background.

Everyone has their own unique experience when it comes to education, and this can affect their opinions on the subject. An audience of teachers is likely to be more familiar with the details of an educational issue and must be approached differently from those who are not familiar with it. People of different ages have different perspectives on issues. For example, parents who have children starting school may feel differently about changes to the kindergarten curriculum than parents of a newborn baby. A person's lifestyle, their job, and where they live, may also affect how they feel about issues. When you make an argument, it is important to keep your audience in mind, and ensure that your claims and evidence will relate to them.

Introductions Count

Your introduction should get the reader interested in the topic and clearly introduce your main argument. An introduction should include a statement that interests the reader. For example, an argument in favor of moving high school starts to later in the day could state:

> *Did you know that a Virginia school district that started the school day an hour earlier saw its students involved in 40 percent more car crashes than a district that started its day an hour later? Believe it or not, these things are connected. There is a way we can reduce car crashes and improve our teenagers' performance at school, and it all relates to when they start their day.*

Consider who is making the argument. For example, a high school teacher may have a very informed perspective on school start times and student's performance.

The Stanford University Sleep Disorders Clinic warns that teens who do not get enough sleep may find it harder to concentrate, resulting in lower grades.

Clincher Conclusions

The conclusion is as important as your introduction. It restates your core argument and claims. Your conclusion should end with a **clincher**. This is a statement that strengthens your argument by capturing the reader's attention right at the end, so that they are more likely to consider all your points and agree with you.

In the argument about moving high school start times, a clincher could state:

Given the data, early school start times clearly harm our teenagers. Starting high schools later in the day will not only improve student grades, but it will also make them and all of us safer.

A clincher can also be a quote or a question that makes the reader think, such as:

If such a simple measure as moving school starts to later in the day could improve students' performance and reduce the number of car accidents, shouldn't we at least test the idea and see how much it benefits students and society?

Choose Your Words

The words you use and how you use them will help persuade people to see and appreciate your point of view. Words can appeal to someone's emotions and strengthen your evidence. For example, referring to sources of facts and statistics will back up your claims. Quoting **qualified** experts can make people more likely to believe you. Words can appeal to people's emotions by emphasizing or stressing things they care about. In the school starts argument, words can emphasize the benefits to teenagers' academic futures and to their safety.

Powerful Words

How effective an argument is depends on the types of words used. **Rhetoric** is the art of using language effectively when writing or speaking. It is usually used in persuasive speaking or writing by appealing to a reader's or listener's emotions.

Persuasive Trio

There are three types of rhetoric: logos, pathos, and ethos.

Logos: Logos uses logic and reason to prove a point. Logos is an ancient Greek word from which we get the word "logic." It uses facts and statistics to support a point. A logical argument backed up with solid facts will help others consider your position, even if they do not agree with it. Here is an example of logos:

> *Plans by the Oregon legislature would raise **corporate** taxes to put $1.4 billion into education, and hire more teachers to reduce class sizes. This would improve the quality of education for all students. Research by the National Education Association shows that this investment would add 23,600 more jobs and boost the economy.*

Pathos: An argument based on pathos appeals to the audience's emotions with personal stories.

Talking about billion-dollar investments distances audience members who cannot see how these numbers relate to a single classroom. However, a story about a student who benefited from the extra time their teacher was able to help them not only appeals to the audience's emotions, but also provides an example to show why the statistics are important. Pathos should be used only to support your claim. It should not be used to confuse or frighten people in order to win an argument. A good example of pathos is:

> *Sarah hated sixth grade. The rooms were too crowded, and the teacher didn't have time for her. The heating didn't work, and the roof leaked. All of these distractions meant that her grades suffered. But things changed over the summer. Workers fixed up the school and added additional rooms. New teachers were hired. When Sarah returned to school, she didn't have to compete with as many classmates for attention. There were after-school programs she could take part in. Now she's eager to prepare for high school.*

How you present your argument is very important. You can engage the audience by speaking clearly and directly to them.

Ethos: Ethos is language that influences a person to trust the speaker. Using reliable sources to build an argument can do this. The person can also tell the audience about his or her experience on the topic. In addition, always respecting the opposing view and presenting it correctly to the audience can establish trust. Here is an example of ethos:

> *In my 25 years in education, I have been a teacher, principal, and school administrator. I've had to deal with the day-to-day operations of schools and balance school budgets. I know firsthand the work teachers put into teaching their students. It's a tough and important job. That is why I believe we need to support education with more funding.*

You can use ethos in an argument by researching and including quotes from qualified professionals or experts.

LOOKING AT LANGUAGE

Read the following statement. Can you identify the rhetoric the author has used?

A study from Northwestern University and the University of California, Berkeley, showed that each 10 percent increase in the money available for low-income students resulted in an equivalent increase in the students' earnings when they became adults. Not only will this increase the taxes they pay, giving back the money the government spent on their education, but it will also offer them better and happier lives—not just for them, but for their children, too.

Which types of rhetoric does the statement use to appeal to the audience? What words or phrases make you think so?

Where Do You Stand?

Read these two arguments about whether students should be allowed to bring cell phones into class. Keep in mind the features of an argument and the power of language. Which argument do you feel is stronger? Why?

Students Should Not Be Allowed to Bring Cell Phones into Class.

Would a teacher allow a student to bring a television into class to watch their favorite show? Would a teacher allow a student to call a friend on the phone and talk to them during class? Then why would anyone expect teachers to allow students to bring mobile devices to class?

Cell phones are distractions. Students pay attention to their phones and not to the teacher. Because of their size, they are difficult for teachers to spot. Their computing abilities make cell phones obvious tools for students to cheat on tests. A study from the group Common Sense Media shows that, of 2,000 middle and high school students in the United States, 35 percent say they have used a cell phone to cheat on a test at least once.

Cell phones and mobile devices have also been platforms for school **cyberbullying** and harassment. Studies from the Cyberbullying

According to British government surveys, 98 percent of British schools have banned cell phones in classrooms.

Research Center show that half of young people experience some form of cyberbullying, and up to 20 percent experience it regularly.

We are not afraid of new technology. We know that computers have enhanced students' education. However, where schools introduce computers, tablets, and other devices into classroom learning, they carefully manage students' access. This is impossible if students bring their own devices into the classroom.

Teachers and school officials face many challenges when teaching students without adding cell phones to the mix. If students want to learn, they need to leave their cell phones behind.

Students Should Be Allowed to Bring Cell Phones into Class.

Cell phones and mobile devices, if properly managed, can be useful tools to help students learn in the classroom. They do not need to be banned.

For teenagers and parents, cell phones are an important tool that helps them keep in touch. Research from Verizon Wireless shows that 95 percent of parents who buy their children a cell phone do so to keep them safe. When children have cell phones at all times, parents can send messages to their children without having to call in and disrupt the school office.

Mobile devices are an opportunity to improve teens' education. Educational learning apps can help them stay on top of and complete classwork. Many apps exist to help students develop better study habits, including **time management** and organization skills. Mobile devices can help teachers add a digital element into their lessons, pointing students to online resources that can improve their learning experience and education.

As new technologies emerge, there are people who fear change. They argue that cell phones distract students from lessons or give them more ways to cheat on tests. However, teachers have had to manage similar problems before mobile devices, and many schools are dealing with these issues without banning cell phones from classrooms. Matthew Lynch, a columnist for the publication the *Tech Edvocate*, advises that teachers establish their expectations for the class early, walk around the classroom to observe students up-close, confiscate misused cell phones if necessary, but also use phones as an educational tool to enhance lessons.

The benefits of mobile devices are so clear that governments such as California and Ontario are spending hundreds of millions of dollars to bring tablet computers into the classroom. As with any other technology, problems can be avoided if teachers manage cell phone use. The future of the classroom could well be in the hands of the students right now.

*In the United States, a Pew Research study showed 73 percent of **Advanced Placement** teachers allowed students to use their cell phones in the classroom to complete assignments.*

CHAPTER 3

SHOULD SCHOOLS TEACH MORE STEM SUBJECTS AND LESS ARTS?

Ever since school became compulsory for children, people have argued over what schools should teach. Since there are only so many hours in the school day, and only so much money available to schools, we cannot expect the education system to teach children everything. So, which should have priority: creative subjects such as arts and music, or subjects such as science and math?

What Do Students Need?

Until the last quarter of the twentieth century, a high school education was enough for most adults to find a job that could support a family. However, the nature of work in North America has changed. Industrial robots, computers, and competition with other countries have reduced the number of **low-skill jobs** available to North Americans, and increased the skills needed for higher-paying jobs. By the 1990s, many people found they needed a university degree to land a good job.

Because technology is becoming more important in our jobs and lives, many people believe that

schools should spend more time teaching STEM subjects. STEM education aims to teach science, math, technology, and engineering in a way that encourages discovery, creativity, and thinking critically. Supporters point to studies showing that, out of 65 education systems around the world, Americans ranked twenty-seventh in math and twentieth in science. Canadians ranked ninth in math and seventh in science. STEM education is needed to improve North America's standing in these fields. They argue that students who participate in STEM education will do better in a variety of jobs, such as accounting, nursing, construction, or computer work.

Art is seen by many as important for early childhood education because it teaches children fine motor control, or using their hands better.

Are Art and Music Useful?

Given that there is only so much schools can teach, some argue that schools should focus on STEM subjects instead of arts programs, such as visual arts (including drawing, painting, and pottery), drama, literature, and music. Even before the current push for more STEM education, fewer schools were offering music because of the high cost of instruments and specialized teaching staff.

Some point out that few artists and musicians make enough money at their crafts to support themselves, so why should schools encourage students to aquire these skills? Others have defended art and music, noting that the skills these subjects build, such as problem-solving, have far wider applications. Because of this, some people suggest that, instead of STEM, schools should use the acronym STEAM, where the "A" stands for art. They argue that art and music are vital components of a good education.

So, what are the arguments for and against teaching more math and sciences and less arts and music?

According to a study by Economic Modeling Specialists International, the average income for STEM jobs in the United States is $38.85/hour, compared to $19.30/hour for all other jobs.

ARTS AND MUSIC

Here are some useful statistics about arts and music in schools:

- According to a 2015 U.S. study, more than 8,000 public schools do not have a music program.
- According to a 2010 survey by Coalition for Music Education in Canada, 10 percent of schools do not have a specialist music teacher, while 26 percent say lack of time puts pressure on music lessons.
- Arts and music are mandatory subjects in Japan, Hungary, and the Netherlands. These countries often rank the highest for math and science test scores.

Schools Should Teach More STEM Subjects and Less Arts.

Tomorrow's work force will be relying more and more on STEM subjects. Computers are changing every **industry**. **Automation** is cutting low-skill jobs, while increasing jobs for those who **program** computers and design equipment. Teaching subjects such as math, science, programming, industrial design, and engineering will help students succeed in these fields, and find better and higher-paying jobs. A Georgetown University study from 2015 notes that students who graduated with an arts or a humanities degree, were more likely to be unemployed than students who graduated with a science or medical degree. The Canadian Office of the Chief Economist notes that the number of STEM-related jobs grew by 24.4 percent over the past decade, compared to 4 percent for other jobs. STEM workers also earned 29 percent more than

workers who were not in STEM-related fields. A study by *USA Today* indicated that 70 percent of low-skilled jobs were at risk of automation over the next 20 years, compared with 8 percent of high-skilled jobs.

If we do not teach more STEM education, we will fall behind other countries that do. Many countries teach students far more science than the United States or Canada. This gives their students more skills to compete for the jobs in technology, invention, and design that many people expect will be more important in the future. A 2015 report from the Organisation for Economic Co-operation and Development (OECD) ranked the 40 most-advanced countries in the world based on their levels of science education. Canada was ranked 22, while the United States ranked 39.

STEM education supporters, such as the Carnegie Foundation, argue that teaching children STEM subjects helps them excel at these subjects when they are older and getting ready to work.

According to researchers at Oxford University, England, people who program, design, install, and repair robots are among the least likely to have their jobs taken over by robots.

Both were below the OECD average. Countries higher up the ranking, such as South Korea, Germany, and Sweden, had more than 28 percent of their university students graduate with degrees in science and engineering, while Canada only had 21 percent, and the United States 16 percent. Because of a lack of qualified workers in the United States, reports the *Wall Street Journal*, 2.5 million STEM jobs are not being filled.

Art and music teach skills students can use while learning math and science, such as creativity, problem solving, and **critical thinking**. However, it costs too much to teach these classes. According to the National Education Music Company, instruments can cost between $600 and $1,500 per student. Sheet music can cost between

$50 and $100 per title. Since 2008, more than 80 percent of U.S. schools have had to cut their budgets. Is it asking too much to teach these expensive courses at the same time as increasing the amount of STEM education?

We can see that the future is bringing more jobs that require students to understand science, technology, engineering, and math. Students who pursue degrees outside these fields face greater difficulty finding work. We owe it to our children to use our schools' budgets most effectively to give them the tools they need to succeed. That means more STEM subjects and less arts and music at school.

Schools Should Not Sacrifice Arts for More STEM Education.

Arts and music are a vital part of a good and balanced education and should not be sacrificed for more STEM education. Even if arts and music are not pursued as careers, learning these subjects gives students essential skills that make it easier to learn other subjects, such as math and science. Researchers at the University of California, Los Angeles, named 62 studies on the benefits students receive from various types of art education. All show that students who learn arts and music develop skills that help them in other subjects. Music teaches scales, intervals, and patterns, all of which are useful in learning concepts in math. Learning an instrument also benefits coordination. Drama helps students express and understand complex issues and emotions, which helps with critical thinking. Visual arts help students improve the appearance and organization of what they write and present. All arts fields help students work together and think creatively, which is important for STEM subjects.

Teaching children just for the jobs that are available right now may not prepare them for the future job market they will encounter. Thanks to changing technology, the job market is changing

Proponents of arts subjects argue that music and theater allow students to be active, making it easier for them to sit at their desks for longer.

at a fast pace. In 2018, the publication *Forbes* noted that jobs such as data entry operator, word processor, and electrical equipment assembler have seen numbers drop in the past decade. During this time, a **generation** of students went through school. For students to be more certain of getting jobs after they graduate, it may not help for them to train for a specific job or career. Instead, people have to be flexible and creative to be able to adapt themselves to different possible jobs. Arts and music help teach these skills. According to the employment website *LinkedIn*,

young people today change jobs four times within their first 10 years after graduation. That is twice the average of people in the previous generation. A 2016 report by the World Economic Forum states that, by 2020, creativity will be one of the three most important skills of any job applicant, something enhanced by arts and music.

Teaching subjects such as arts and music can be expensive. It is true that schools have only limited budgets. Critics of arts teaching might suggest that teamwork, creativity, and critical thinking can all be taught in math and science classes. However, these skills are more effectively taught by arts and music. It is no coincidence that some of our greatest scientists were also great artists and musicians. Italy's Leonardo da Vinci was not just an artist, but an inventor, a mathematician, and an explorer of biology, medicine, and geology. Scientist Albert Einstein played classical music on his violin while brainstorming.

We agree that children need a good education to find fulfilling jobs, and that is why arts and music need to be taught in schools. Not only do these subjects teach children skills that help them understand STEM subjects, but encouraging children to be creative will help them adapt to future jobs that we cannot predict. We owe our children a good education, and that is one that includes arts and music.

Statistics from the U.S. SAT scores show that students taking music classes score on average 53 points higher on the verbal portion of the test and 39 points higher on the math portion.

STATE YOUR CASE

When it comes to any issue, you need to look at arguments on both sides before you decide where you stand. When you evaluate the arguments for and against schools teaching more sciences and less arts, remember the features of effective arguments. Which side's argument do you think is stronger? Why do you think so? Give reasons for your answers. Use the "In Summary: For and Against" list to help you figure out your decision, and state your own case.

IN SUMMARY: FOR AND AGAINST

For Teaching More STEM Subjects and Less Arts

Tomorrow's work force will be relying more and more on STEM subjects.

- Computers and robots are changing every industry. A study by *USA Today* suggests that 70 percent of low-skilled jobs may be lost to robots over the next 20 years.
- Teaching skills such as programming, industrial design, and engineering will help students find better and higher-paying jobs.
- Students who graduate with an arts or a humanities degree are more likely to be unemployed than students who graduate with a science or medical degree.
- The Canadian Office of the Chief Economist notes that the number of STEM-related jobs grew by 24.4 percent over the past decade, compared to 4 percent for other jobs.

If we do not teach more STEM education, we will fall behind other countries that do.

- A 2015 OECD report ranked Canada as 22 and the United States as 39 out of the 40 most-advanced countries, based on their levels of science education.
- Because of a lack of qualified workers in the United States, 2.5 million STEM jobs are not being filled.

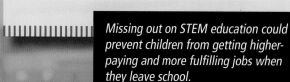

Missing out on STEM education could prevent children from getting higher-paying and more fulfilling jobs when they leave school.

Against Teaching Less Arts

Arts and music are a vital part of a good and balanced education.

- Music and arts classes enhance creativity, encourage students to express ideas and emotions, and help students to work together.
- Music lessons help with coordination and teach scales, intervals, and patterns, which are useful in learning concepts in math.
- Drama helps students understand complex issues and emotions.
- Visual arts help students improve the appearance and organization of what they write and present.

Teaching children just for the jobs that are available right now may not prepare them for the future job market they will encounter.

- Changing technology means that the job market is rapidly changing. It is not always useful to train for a specific career.
- Young people today change jobs four times within their first 10 years after graduation.
- A 2016 report by the World Economic Forum states that, by 2020, creativity will be one of the three most important skills of any job applicant. Learning arts and music help with flexibility and creativity.
- Some of our greatest scientists, including Albert Einstein, were also great artists and musicians.

Can art and science work together? The organization STEM to STEAM and schools such as the Rhode Island School of Design argue that art is a vital part of helping students learn the other subjects of STEM.

CHAPTER 4

SHOULD SCHOOLS STOP ASSIGNING HOMEWORK?

People have argued about homework from the moment teachers started assigning it. As far back as 1901, the California legislature banned homework for students from kindergarten to grade eight. Some people think that children, particularly young ones, should work at school but play at home. However, many others believe that homework is a vital part of a good education.

Practice Makes Perfect

Teachers assign homework to help students review the things they have been taught. Allowing students to practice exercises at their own speed may help them learn and understand the material better. Having more chances to practice a new skill helps students master it.

In the United States, homework has been seen as especially important in the last half of the twentieth century, because the U.S. government worried that its schools were falling behind those of other developed nations. Today, the National Education Association advocates the "10-minute rule." They believe that children should be assigned 10 minutes of homework per grade per night. This means that a second grader would have 20 minutes of homework every night, while a senior in high school would have 2 hours per night. However, some schools assign more than this, while others assign less. A survey by the University of Phoenix College of Education suggests that, in the most extreme cases, high school students in the United States can receive as much as 17.5 hours of homework a week, or 2.5 hours each night.

There have been different views on homework over the years. In the 1950s and 1980s, it was seen as a way to improve the education system. In the 1960s, educators and parents argued that homework was keeping children from playing together and exercising outdoors.

A new approach to homework may be to do it at school. In recent years, a small number of schools have tried a new technique called "the flipped classroom." In this arrangement, students watch a teacher's lesson or lecture online at home. They then bring their questions and their homework assignments to school the next day. There, they work with their peers to finish the assignments, and get help from teachers as they encounter problems.

Arguments About Homework

For many students, homework is a source of stress. It is also stressful for parents because many argue with their children about doing their homework. Parents' groups have argued with schools and each other about the merits of assigning homework. They note studies that suggest that homework is not as effective in early grades as it is in later grades. Some educators are also questioning how effective homework actually is in students' performance, while others note that taking work home is a fact of life in many adult jobs.

Homework can be used by teachers to show parents what their children are learning, and get them to help. This assumes the parent is available to help, however, which is not always the case.

So, what are the arguments for and against schools stopping homework?

HOMEWORK STATISTICS

Here are some interesting statistics about homework:

- According to a 2014 Stanford University study, 56 percent of students considered homework their top source of stress.
- A 2012 study by tutoring company Oxford Learning found that 72 percent of parents felt homework was a major source of stress.
- A 2013 study of 15-year-olds by the Organisation for Economic Cooperation and Development (OECD) found that students from China received the most homework, averaging 14 hours per week. Canadians and Americans got an average of 6 hours per week. Finland and South Korea received just 3 hours per week. A 2015 OECD study of education systems ranked Finland first, South Korea fifth, Canada seventh, and the United States twenty-fifth.

Schools Should Stop Assigning Homework.

Schools should stop assigning homework because it negatively affects students' health and is not an effective learning tool. Schools currently assign too much homework, which adds to the stress students feel. Adding hours of homework to students' days can make them feel tired and overworked. In the few hours between returning from school and going to bed, homework has to compete with daily chores, extracurricular activities, interacting with family, personal time, and sleep. Having too much homework may lead students to drop extracurricular activities, stop seeing friends and family, and cut down on activities they enjoy. These are all activities that are essential for the well-being and development of children and teens. A 2014 Stanford University study of 4,317 high school students found that 56 percent considered homework to be a main source of stress. When the students were asked about the impact homework had on their health, many said they had lost sleep due to homework. Many said homework led them to spend less time with friends or less time playing. Others said they felt the amount of homework they were given was linked to experiencing health issues such as headaches, exhaustion, stomach problems, and weight loss. When students are given little or no homework, they have more time to relax and are therefore happier and better able to learn when they return to the classroom. Finland, which the OECD rates as having one of the world's best education systems, assigns one of the lowest amounts of homework: just 3 hours per week on average for high school students.

Homework is not as effective a learning tool as other teaching methods. Most homework is done at home, alone. This means that students cannot ask for help when they come across concepts they do not understand. When students do not understand their homework, it does not help learning. Instead, it may reinforce confusion. In the flipped-classroom method, students watch online tutorials from their teacher while they are at home. Then, in the classroom, students do their

The Stanford study also found that fewer than one percent said that homework was not a stressor.

written or practical "homework," with teachers and peers around to help. Schools that have taken this approach have seen improvements. When Clintondale High School in Clinton Township, Michigan, which had a high failure rate among students, adopted the flipped classroom in 2010, failure rates went down by one-third.

There are studies, such as a 2006 report from Duke University, North Carolina, showing that students who complete homework regularly are more likely to succeed at school. However, these studies can be looked at another way: just because someone does well at school does not mean that homework helped them succeed. It is equally possible that they finish their homework more easily because they learn quickly at school.

Homework is a source of stress for students and parents alike. Students lose sleep with too much homework, and they stop spending time with parents and friends. The benefits of homework are also questionable, with countries such as Finland showing that you do not need a lot of homework for students to have a good education. Given that better educational tools exist, it is time to put the pencils down on homework.

The CDC says that children and teens should spend an hour or more each day doing physical activity to stay healthy. Too much homework may cut into that important time.

Schools Should Continue to Assign Homework.

Homework teaches skills that are not learned as easily in the classroom. Homework allows students to work **independently** and to learn to manage their time. By allowing them to choose where and when to do their work, while meeting regular deadlines, they will be better prepared to join the workforce as adults. A 2013 study by Concordia University of Portland, Oregon, identified the four important qualities taught by homework as: responsibility, time management, perseverance, and **self-esteem**. In its report, it states that "perseverance has garnered a lot of attention as an essential skill for successful students. Regular accomplishments like finishing homework build self-esteem, which aids students' mental and physical health."

Homework is an important tool to show teachers that students are fully understanding what they are being taught. A teacher can only do so much within a busy classroom. Other than tests and asking questions, homework is one of the main tools teachers have to see whether students have understood and are able to apply the methods and facts they have been taught in class. Homework helps teachers see when a student is falling behind on their lessons, so they can offer extra help. Many studies, including a 2014 report for the state of Victoria in Australia on the effectiveness of homework in helping students learn, have shown a link between assigning homework and teachers being able to respond to students' needs. They all point out that a key part of this relationship is **feedback**. Students performed better on tests when teachers read their homework, gave praise for things done well, and offered **constructive criticism** for mistakes.

The Association for Supervision and Curriculum Development (ASCD) recommends educational games, creative challenges, and applying classroom lessons to real-life situations as ways to increase student enthusiasm.

Many parents and children state that homework is a main source of stress and argument. However, rather than dropping homework, perhaps parents should be given more guidance on managing homework and discussions around it. Parents are vital to a child's education, and homework is the main way that parents can engage with their children's studies. Parents can support their children by reviewing lessons and making sure that homework is completed. Education studies, including a 2005 report from the U.S. Department of Education, showed that parents who encouraged children to do their homework—without doing the work for them—helped their children do better at school, including increasing their test scores. The U.S. Department of Education states that homework can "provide opportunities for parents to see what their children are learning in school and help families communicate with their children and school staff."

Few people like to do homework, but few people like to do household chores, either, and we know how important such work is. Homework is too effective an educational tool to leave behind. It helps students develop skills such as time management and perseverance, can build self-esteem, and help with understanding the lessons taught in school. Homework also aids teachers in monitoring students' progress, and helps parents engage with what their children are learning. With all of this evidence, it is clear that homework is vital to a successful education.

Without homework, teachers would have to rely on quizzes, exams, and interviews to determine how well students were learning the curriculum.

STATE YOUR CASE

When it comes to any issue, you need to look at arguments on both sides before you decide where you stand. When you evaluate the arguments for and against ending homework, remember the features of effective arguments. Which side's argument do you think is stronger? Why do you think so? Give reasons for your answers. Use the "In Summary: For and Against" list to help you figure out your decision, and state your own case.

IN SUMMARY: FOR AND AGAINST

For Ending Homework

Schools currently assign too much homework, which stresses students and leads to unhealthy behavior.

- Hours of homework can make students tired, overworked, and stressed.
- A 2014 Stanford University study found that 56 percent of students considered homework to be a main source of stress.
- Having too much homework may lead students to stop doing chores, stop seeing friends and family, and cut down on extracurricular activities that are essential for well-being and development.
- Finland, which the OECD rates as having one of the best education systems in the world, assigns one of the lowest amounts of homework in the world: just 3 hours per week on average for high school students.

Homework is not as effective a learning tool as other teaching methods.

- When doing homework, students cannot ask for help from teachers or peers.
- When students do not understand their homework, it may reinforce confusion.
- When Clintondale High School in Michigan, which had a high failure rate among students, adopted the flipped-classroom in 2010, failure rates went down by one-third.

A barrier to the flipped-classroom model is that some children do not have access to technology at home to make it work.

Against Ending Homework

Homework teaches skills that are not learned as easily in the classroom.

- Homework allows students to work independently and to learn to manage their time. These skills prepare students to join the workforce as adults.
- A 2013 study by Concordia University of Portland, Oregon, identified the four important qualities taught by homework as: responsibility, time management, perseverance, and self-esteem.

A 2014 report by the University of Reading, United Kingdom, found that "[teacher] feedback can improve a student's confidence, self-awareness and enthusiasm for learning."

Homework is an important tool to show teachers that students are fully understanding what they are being taught.

- Homework is one of the main tools teachers have to see whether students have understood what they are taught in class.
- If homework reveals a gap in a student's understanding, teachers can offer extra help.
- A 2014 report for the state of Victoria in Australia showed a link between assigning homework and teachers being able to respond to students' needs.
- The U.S. Department of Education states that homework can "provide opportunities for parents to see what their children are learning in school."

CHAPTER 5

SHOULD SCHOOLS REDUCE THE TWO-MONTH SUMMER BREAK?

Most students look forward to the long summer vacation in July and August. It is a time for relaxation, pursuing sports and other interests, family time, and even adventures. Yet some people think the summer break is too long and is damaging children's education. They think that breaks from school should be evenly spaced throughout the year.

The long summer break is not just a feature of North American schools. At least 89 other countries have long summer breaks, including European nations such as the United Kingdom, France, and Germany. However, some schools in North America and around the world adopt a model in which students have regular one- or two-week breaks throughout the year. They argue that this allows students regular time off to relax and connect with their families, without the drawbacks of a long summer break.

Mysterious Beginnings

The summer break has been a part of the school year for as long as there has been public education, starting in the mid-nineteenth century. However, there is no clear reason why the tradition of a summer break started. Many people believe that the long break was first set up to give children time to work on family farms, but other evidence does not support this. In fact, in the nineteenth century, **rural** schools would often break during harvest–in fall, but teach classes through the summer.

In the early days of public education, many educators looked at the brain as though it were a muscle that, if overworked, could lead to injury. Educators argued that children should spend their summers with their families. There were also practical concerns. In the days before air conditioning, it was often too hot to be indoors during summer.

A Different World

Times have changed. Today, many schools are air conditioned. Since few North American parents work in farming, most jobs do not follow a

Most schools in North America have followed the summer break tradition for almost two centuries. Many are resistant to change.

seasonal pattern. Some people suggest that the summer break should be shortened, spreading the vacation weeks through the year. This would stop a problem they call "**backsliding**," where students returning from the summer vacation have forgotten what they were taught before they left. People also point out that students forget the schedules, rules, and expectations of school classrooms over the summer. As a result, teachers must spend instructional time reviewing classroom behavior at the start of each year. Reducing the length of school breaks will mean that students remain prepared to learn throughout the year.

According to a survey posted by the New York Times in 2012, the average American family spends $601 on summer activities per child. Wealthy families spend $1,116 per child.

However, keeping schools open year-round would disrupt the business of companies offering summer camps and activities for children. It also affects industries that depend on students working summer jobs. People also argue that keeping schools open year-round would increase maintenance and janitorial costs. Today, schools offering year-round schooling, with shortened summer breaks and longer vacations during the rest of the year, can be found in 45 American states and across Canada. Experts are watching how the two models perform, and the results of their findings may bring changes to school schedules.

So, what are the arguments for and against shortening the summer break?

SCHOOLS AND SUMMER BREAKS

Here are some useful facts about summer breaks:

- Nearly 3,700 schools across the United States and 150 in Canada offer year-round learning, with shortened summer breaks.
- According to the U.S. Bureau of Labor Statistics, teenagers age 16 to 19 represented 4.5 percent of America's labor force in July 2016.
- The U.S. Travel Association states that summer vacation travel brought in $2.1 trillion in 2014.

Schools Should Reduce the Two-Month Summer Break.

To benefit students' health and education, schools should reduce the two-month summer break and spread shorter breaks evenly through the school year. Unless students are enrolled in educational activities during the summer vacation, they tend to lose skills they learn before the summer break. Educational summer activities often come at a high cost, meaning that students who come from wealthier families are at an advantage compared to those who come from families who cannot afford to enroll them in summer activities. Public education is meant to give every student the ability to succeed, regardless of their parents' income. The summer break can cause issues of fairness in education. A 2012 study by McMaster University, Ontario, found that educational camps, family trips, and extra reading books available to children of wealthier families gave their education a "summer surge" not available to children

from poorer families. Although educational activities can help some students retain skills during summer break, as a whole, students tend to lose skills over the break. Studies conducted by the John Hopkins Research Institute, the RAND Institute, and the University of California, Berkeley, illustrate a trend called "backsliding." Standardized test scores of students taken before and after summer vacation show that many lose as much as a month of grade-level skills during the break, with math skills in particular seeing the greatest drop.

A school schedule with ten months of school and two months off can also negatively affect the health of students and school staff. Long semesters with little time for relaxation can cause stress and burn out. Spreading vacation time into short breaks throughout the year gives students

Supporters of year-round schooling suggest that shorter periods of school and more frequent breaks can keep students refreshed and better able to learn.

A 2013 survey of 500 teachers by the U.S. National Summer Learning Association found that two-thirds of teachers felt they spent three to four weeks teaching students what they had forgotten over the summer.

and teachers more frequent time off, allowing them to remain well, enthusiastic, and able to teach and learn to the best of their ability. Roberta Bondar Elementary School in Brampton, Ontario, switched to the year-round schedule. Students at the school say they found the old schedule, which had a two-month summer, tougher than the year-round schedule. One student said, "It's actually really tiring because throughout the semester, you actually need more breaks." Similar findings have been reported in the 150 other Canadian schools that offer a year-round schedule. Students' physical fitness can also suffer because of the 2-month summer. A 2007 report by the *American Journal of Public Health* showed that backsliding affects physical education, as children gain weight more rapidly when they are out of school during summer vacation.

It is argued that a year-round schedule may increase school maintenance costs, as schools normally shut down completely in the long summer break, saving the costs of janitors, cleaners, and air conditioning. However, this relatively small cost increase would be worth the benefits to students and teachers. The research and real experiences of students show that regular breaks help students be healthier and more ready to learn throughout the year. Teachers are more refreshed and, when students are prepared and ready to learn, can spend more classroom time focused on educational activities. A year-round school schedule allows students to make the most of their education.

Given the harm that the long summer vacation does to students' education and health, especially for students from poorer families, it makes no sense to keep the summer vacation tradition alive. Year-round schooling improves students' learning and keeps them refreshed throughout the year. It is time to replace the old system with a schedule that reflects today's realities.

Schools Should Not Reduce the Two-Month Summer Break.

Taking away the summer vacation will complicate the lives of teachers, parents, and summer job employers by making it difficult for teens to enter the workforce, harming business owners, and removing the chance for students to build new skills. The summer vacation has been a fact of the school year for nearly two centuries. Many families plan their vacations around it, have existing summer day-care arrangements, and do not want the current system to change. A survey by the American Automobile Association showed that 35 percent of American families planned to travel during summer vacation in 2017. In some American schools where year-round schooling was tried, parents complained about it. For example, schools in Los Angeles tested year-round schooling in the late 1980s. After testing the schedule, it gave schools the option to choose year-round schooling or go back to the old schedule, with a two-month summer. All but one of its 544 schools chose to bring back the long summer break.

Many businesses would be negatively affected by the removal of a summer break. Businesses offering childcare, summer camps, or other summer activities would lose the income that the summer break brings. A number of industries, particularly tourism, depend on students working summer jobs. A national survey by the website *CareerBuilder.com* found that 41 percent of companies planned to hire seasonal workers for the summer of 2017. Many governments offer summer jobs to high school students as part of programs to help young people gain job experience.

Shortening the summer vacation would make it harder for teenagers to gain experiences that increase their life skills. The long summer break is often a time for teenagers to take short-term jobs that earn them money and give them workplace experience they can show to future employers. Colleges and universities also tend

According to a study by the youth organization 4-H, teenagers hired as summer camp counselors learn about leadership and responsibility in ways they might not have learned at school.

Organizations like Youth Exchange and Study use the summer break to send students to different countries to learn about other cultures.

to look for summer work experience as a sign of committed and hard-working students. Spreading out vacation weeks throughout the year shortens the big block of time that makes this possible. According to the U.S. Bureau of Labor Statistics (BLS), 33 percent of teenagers had summer jobs in 2015. Other students take summer **internships** or **volunteer** work to gain useful experience.

Studies by John Hopkins Research Institute, the RAND Institute, and the University of California, Berkeley, show that some children do fall backward with some of their skills during the long summer break. However, with good teaching, these children can soon be brought back up to speed. To provide this good teaching, many teachers use the summer vacation to improve their own skills by reading background material or taking courses, and to get ahead on setting classwork for the next semester.

Summer vacation is a tradition. Parents have developed a pattern around it: They are used to signing children up for day camps and organizing extended vacations over these months. Businesses, large and small, depend on the long school break to provide services such as childcare to families. Many students use summer vacation to gain experiences that will help them after they graduate. Reducing the summer break would disrupt this rhythm. There is a saying that, if something is not broken, you should not try to fix it. Summer vacation is not broken, so we should not change it.

STATE YOUR CASE

When it comes to any issue, you need to look at arguments on both sides before you decide where you stand. When you evaluate the arguments for and against reducing the length of the summer vacation and spreading breaks evenly through the year, remember the features of effective arguments. Which side's argument do you think is stronger? Why do you think so? Give reasons for your answers. Use the "In Summary: For and Against" list to help you figure out your decision, and state your own case.

IN SUMMARY: FOR AND AGAINST

For Reducing the Summer Break

The long summer vacation harms students' education by causing them to forget skills they learned throughout the year.

- Unless students are enrolled in educational activities during the summer vacation, they tend to backslide, or lose skills they learned before the summer break.
- Standardized test scores of students taken before and after summer vacation show that many lose as much as a month of grade-level skills during the break.
- Studies have shown that a long summer break negatively affects families with lower incomes, because they cannot afford to enroll children in educational summer experiences. This can give students from wealthier families an unfair advantage.

The ten-month on, two-month off school schedule can be harmful to the health of students and school staff.

- Spreading short breaks throughout the year can help reduce stress and keep students and teachers well and enthusiastic.
- Findings in 150 Canadian schools offering year-round schooling were that students prefer regular, shorter breaks.
- A 2007 report from the *American Journal of Public Health* showed that children gained weight more rapidly when they are out of school during summer vacation.

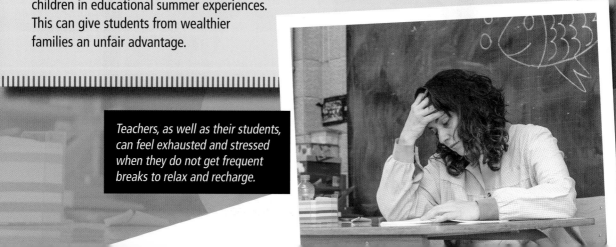

Teachers, as well as their students, can feel exhausted and stressed when they do not get frequent breaks to relax and recharge.

Against Reducing the Summer Break

Taking away the summer vacation will complicate the lives of families and harm business owners.

- Many families plan their vacations around the break, have existing daycare arrangements, and do not want to change. When some Los Angeles schools tried year-round schooling, parents complained.
- A survey by the American Automobile Association showed that 35 percent of U.S. families planned to travel during summer vacation in 2017.
- Industries such as tourism depend on students working summer jobs.

Shortening the summer vacation would make it harder for teenagers to gain experiences that increase their life skills and allow them to earn money.

- Spreading out vacation weeks throughout the year shortens the big block of time that makes it possible for teenagers to take summer jobs, volunteer, or take internships.
- Colleges and universities look for summer work experience as a sign of committed and hard-working students.
- In 2015, 33 percent of high school students improved their life skills by taking a summer job.

Each year at the end of the summer break, the financial company Deloitte estimates that U.S. parents spend $27 billion on back-to-school shopping. This benefits small and large businesses.

BIBLIOGRAPHY

Education Today and Tomorrow

"4 Big Problems Created by the Standardized Testing Craze." Fishtree, January 19, 2017. www.fishtree.com/blog/4-big-problems-created-by-the-standardized-testing-craze

"Pros & Cons of Standardized Tests." GradePower Learning, June 22, 2017. gradepowerlearning.com/pros-cons-standardized-tests

Walker, Tim. "Survey: 70 Percent Of Educators Say State Assessments Not Developmentally Appropriate." NEA Today, February 18, 2016, https://neatoday.org/2016/02/18/standardized-tests-not-developmentally-appropriate

What Makes an Argument?

"AASM Position: Delay Middle School, High School Start Times." American Academy of Sleep Medicine, April 14, 2017. https://aasm.org/aasm-position-delaying-middle-school-high-school-start-times-is-beneficial-to-students

"Argument: Claims, Reasons, Evidence." Department of Communication University of Pittsburgh, 2017. www.comm.pitt.edu/argument-claims-reasons-evidence

Aston, Jenna. "Computers in the Classroom: Desktop vs. Laptop vs. Tablet." Stone Group, September 22, 2017. www.stonegroup.co.uk/computers-in-the-classroom

Chalabi, Mona. "American Kids Will Spend an Average of 943 Hours in Elementary School This Year." FiveThirtyEight, September 4, 2014. www.fivethirtyeight.com/features/american-kids-will-spend-an-average-of-943-hours-in-elementary-school-this-year

Chen, Stephanie. "In a Wired World, Children Unable to Escape Cyberbullying." CNN, October 5, 2010. www.cnn.com/2010/LIVING/10/04/youth.cyberbullying.abuse/index.html

"Cyber Bullying Statistics." Bullying Statistics, July 7, 2015. www.bullyingstatistics.org/content/cyber-bullying-statistics.html

"Constructing an Argument." Massey University, February 8, 2018. http://owll.massey.ac.nz/study-skills/constructing-an-argument.php

"Eight Major Obstacles to Delaying School Start Times." National Sleep Foundation, 2018. sleepfoundation.org/sleep-news/eight-major-obstacles-delaying-school-start-times

"Examples of Ethos, Logos, and Pathos." Your

Dictionary. http://examples.yourdictionary.com/examples-of-ethos-logos-and-pathos.html

Girard, Patrick. "What Are Arguments?—Logical and Critical Thinking. University of Auckland." FutureLearn, 2017. www.futurelearn.com/courses/logical-and-critical-thinking/0/steps/9137

Gonchar, Michael. "200 Prompts for Argumentative Writing." The New York Times, February 4, 2014. https://learning.blogs.nytimes.com/2014/02/04/200-prompts-for-argumentative-writing

"The Universal Declaration of Human Rights." Claiming Human Rights, January 4, 2010. www.claiminghumanrights.org/udhr_article_26.html

"IPads for Winnipeg Students: The Pros and Cons of High-Tech Learning." CTVNews, September 5, 2013. www.ctvnews.ca/health/ipads-for-winnipeg-students-the-pros-and-cons-of-high-tech-learning-1.1438691

"Later School Start Times: Lazy or Legit?" The Scope, March 16, 2015. https//healthcare.utah.edu/the-scope/shows.php?shows=0_gfpodzir

"How to Manage Cell Phone Use in Your Classroom." The Tech Edvocate, March 19, 2017. www.thetechedvocate.org/how-to-manage-cell-phone-use-in-your-classroom

Martin, Andrew. "How Technology Affects Children's Learning." Psychlopaedia, November 17, 2017. https://psychlopaedia.org/learning-and-development/technology-affects-childrens-learning

McConville, Emily. "Why Banning Cellphones in Schools Misses the Point," Bates College. March 23, 2018. www.bates.edu/news/2018/03/23/why-banning-cellphones-in-schools-misses-the-point

Pryor, Jim. "What Is an Argument?" Philosophical Terms and Methods, January 10, 2006. www.jimpryor.net/teaching/vocab/argument.html

Schulten, Katherine. "10 Ways to Teach Argument-Writing" The New York Times, October 5, 2017. www.nytimes.com/2017/10/05/learning/lesson-plans/10-ways-to-teach-argument-writing-with-the-new-york-times.html

Singh, Kishore. "Education Is a Basic Human Right." The Guardian, April 23, 2015. www.theguardian.com/global-development/2015/apr/23/education-is-a-basic-human-right-why-

private-schools-must-be-resisted

"Cell Phones in the Classroom: Learning Tool of Distraction." Oxford Learning, December 29, 2017. www.oxfordlearning.com/should-cell-phones-be-allowed-classrooms

Smith, Kelly. "Research Links Later School Start Times to Benefits for Teens." Star Tribune, March, 13 2014. www.startribune.com/minn-study-later-school-start-boosts-grades-attendance-moods/249975531

"Teen Car Crashes Linked to Early School Start Times." Live Science, April 15, 2011. www.livescience.com/35620-teen-car-crash-early-school-start-times.html

"The Witching Hour." The Economist, May 28, 2015. www.economist.com/united-states/2015/05/28/the-witching-hour

Tower, Anna "What Is a Clincher at the End of Your Essay?" Pen & the Pad, June 13, 2017. https://penandthepad.com/clincher-end-essay-3995.html

Turabian, Kate L., Student's Guide to Writing College Papers, 4th ed. (Chicago: University of Chicago Press, 2010), p. 18.

Wallace, Kelly. "High-Tech Cheating on the Rise at Schools." CBS News, 17 June 2009. www.cbsnews.com/news/high-tech-cheating-on-the-rise-at-schools

Weida, Stacey, and Stolley, Karl. "Using Rhetorical Devices for Persuasion." Purdue Online Writing Lab, March 11, 2013. https://owl.english.purdue.edu/owl/resource/588/04/

"What Is an Argument?" Critical Thinking Web, 2018. https://philosophy.hku.hk/think/arg/arg.php

Should Schools Teach More STEM Subjects and Less Arts?

Barack, Lauren. "The Business of K12 Music Education." District Administration, September 21, 2015. www.districtadministration.com/article/business-k12-music-education

"Singapore Tops Latest OECD PISA Global Education Survey." OECD, June 16, 2016. www.oecd.org/education/singapore-tops-latest-oecd-pisa-global-education-survey.htm

Elpus, Kenneth. The Status of Music Education in United States Public Schools—2017. (Reston, VA, Give a Note Foundation, 2017.)

Gray, Alex. "The 10 Skills You Need to

Thrive in the Fourth Industrial Revolution." World Economic Forum, January 19, 2016. www.weforum.org/agenda/2016/01/the-10-skills-you-need-to-thrive-in-the-fourth-industrial-revolution

Greene, Jay P., et al. "Arts Education Matters: We Know, We Measured It." *Education Week*, December 2, 2004. www.edweek.org/ew/articles/2014/12/03/13greene.h34.html

Hefling, Kimberly. "Schools Brace for More Budget Cuts." *NBCNews.com*. October 24, 2011. www.nbcnews.com/id/45019433/ns/us_news-life/t/schools-brace-more-budget-cuts

Dyer. M. Christine. "Reinvesting in Arts Education: Winning America's Future through Creative Schools." The President's Committee on the Arts and the Humanities, May 2011. http://americansforhearts.org/sites/defaultfilesReinvestinginArtsEdu.pdf.

"Fast Facts Tool Provides Quick Answers to Many Education Questions." National Center for Education Statistics. https://nces.ed.gov/fastfacts/display.asp?id=158

Weinberger, Norman M. "The Music in Our Minds." Center for the Neurobiology of Learning and Memory, University of California. Accessed February 25, 2014. https://nmw.bio.uci.edu/publications/Weinberger,%201998e.pdf

Wolfe, Edward. "Scientists Who Were Also Accomplished Artists, Writers, Musicians." WolfeMusicEd Blog, October 23, 2015. https://blog.wolfemusiced.com/scientists-who-were-also-accomplished-artists-writers-musicians.htm

Should Schools Stop Assigning Homework?

"Does Your Child Struggle with Homework?" Oxford Learning, September 16, 2016. www.oxfordlearning.com/does-your-child-struggle-with-homework

"Duke Study: Homework Helps Students Succeed in School, as Long as There Isn't Too Much." Duke Today, March 7, 2006. https://today.duke.edu/2006/03/homework.html

Earp, Jo. "Does Homework Contribute to Student Success?" ACER, September 11, 2014. www.teachermagazine.com.au/articles/does-homework-contribute-to-student-success

Fuglei, Monica. "The Homework Debate: How Homework Benefits Students." Concordia University, Portland, April 6, 2018. education.cu-portland.edu/blog/classroom-resources/the-homework-debate-benefits-of-homework

"History of Homework." *SFGate*, December 19, 1999. www.sfgate.com/news/article/HISTORY-OF-HOMEWORK-3053660.php

Hite, Emily, "Excessive Homework for High-Performing High Schoolers Could Be Harmful, Study Finds." March 11, 2014. scopeblog.stanford.edu/2014/03/11/excessive-homework-for-high-performing-high-schoolers-could-be-harmful-study-finds

Kohli, Sonali. "Students in These Countries Spend the Most Time Doing Homework." Quartz, December 12, 2014. qz.com/311360/students-in-these-countries-spend-the-most-time-doing-homework

Templin, Jacob. "When This School Got Rid of Homework, It Saw a Dramatic Outcome." NationSwell, November 10, 2014. https://nationswell.com/michigan-clintondale-high-school-flipped-classroom-success

Wallace, Kelly. "Children Have Three Times Too Much Homework, Study Finds." CNN, August 12, 2015. www.cnn.com/2015/08/12/health/homework-elementary-school-study/index.html

Should Schools Reduce the Two-Month Summer Break?

"The Summer Slump: Do Kids Backslide during Summer Vacation?" *Psychology Today*, July 24, 2017. www.psychologytoday.com/ca/blog/evidence-based-living/201707/the-summer-slump-do-kids-backslide-during-summer-vacation

Brown, Louise. "Summer Widens Rich/Poor Learning Gap." Thestar.com, Toronto Star, July 25, 2012. www.thestar.com/yourtoronto/education/2012/07/25/summer_widens_richpoor_learning_gap.html

Clarke, Conor. "Why We Should Get Rid of Summer Vacation." The *Atlantic*, June 7, 2009. www.theatlantic.com/politics/archive/2009/06/why-we-should-get-rid-of-summer-vacation/18902

"Costs and Benefits of the Year-Round Calendar System." Hanover Research, April 19, 2013. www.hanoverresearch.com/insights-blog/costs-and-benefits-of-the-year-round-calendar-system

Dell'Antonia, Kj. "$16 Billion: The Cost of Summer." The *New York Times,* June 27, 2012. parenting.blogs.nytimes.com/2012/06/27/16-billion-the-cost-of-summer

Fleming, Nora. "After Summer, Teachers Spend a Month Reteaching Students." Education Week—Teacher Beat, June 14, 2013. www.ewa.org/key-coverage/after-summer-teachers-spend-month-reteaching-students

Ireland, Nicole. "Back to School? For Some Canadian Kids, That Was Weeks Ago." *CBCnews*, August 31, 2016. www.cbc.ca/news/canada/back-to-school-year-round-classes-1.3741029

Seymour, Chloe. "Are Year-Round Schools in Michigan's Future?" InspirED Michigan, November 14, 2014. www.inspiredmichigan.com/features/11.14featureyearround.aspx

Von Drehle, David. "The Case Against Summer Vacation." *Time*, July 22, 2010. https://content.time.com/time/magazine/article/0,9171,2005863,00.html

Walker, Jesse. "The War on Summer Vacation." Reason, June 6, 2013. https://reason.com/blog/2013/06/06/the-war-on-summer-vacation

GLOSSARY

Please note: Some **boldfaced** words are defined where they appear in the text.

Advanced Placement A program in the United States and Canada that offers college-level education to high school students

apprenticeships Training programs in which people learn from others who have particular skills

arithmetic The branch of mathematics dealing with numbers, counting, and calculation

audience Spectators, listeners, or readers

automation Replacing human labor with machines

backsliding When students returning from the summer vacation have forgotten what they were taught before they left

compulsory When you have no choice but to do something

constructive criticism Criticism that is useful and helpful

corporate Belonging to a large business

credible Believable or convincing

critical thinking Evaluating something to form a well-reasoned opinion or judgment on it

curriculum The subjects that teachers have to teach students at school

cyberbullying Harassing someone online by sending or posting insulting messages or images

developing world A term often used by the United Nations and other organizations to describe countries where things such as average income, the strength of the economy, infrastructure such as roads, and poverty, education, and health care, are lower in comparison to "developed" countries, such as those in Europe and North America

evaluating Analyzing something carefully to make a judgment about it

evidence Anything, such as data or statistics, that proves or disproves something

extracurricular Something that takes place outside normal school hours and is not part of the school curriculum, such as team sports

feedback Information on progress and tips for improvement

gender The roles of male or female in society

generation All the people in a group or country who are of a similar age, especially when they are considered to have the same experiences or attitudes

human right A basic right (such as the right to liberty, or freedom) that many societies believe every person should have

independently To do something on your own without help from others

industry Specific types of businesses that make goods in factories or offer services

internships Programs of temporary, supervised work in a particular field in order to gain practical experience

learning disabilities Disorders or conditions that affect someone's ability to learn easily

logic A system of thinking and understanding things. Logic follows statements and facts that are known to be true.

low-skill jobs Jobs that do not require a lot of extra education to perform

melatonin A hormone, or chemical, found in the body that is used in response to darkness, helping people to sleep

persuasively In a convincing manner that may make somebody agree with you

program (verb) Writing code that instructs the work or functions of computer applications or programs

public education A school system run by the government and funded by taxes

qualified Having knowledge and expertise in an area, usually as a result

of education and experience

rural In the countryside

seasonal Occurring during a certain season

self-esteem How people feel about themselves

simulators Devices that artificially create the effect of being in certain conditions

sleep cycles The natural patterns of sleeping and waking

standardized When something is made to match other things. A standardized test is one in which all children of a certain age write the same test set out by the government.

statistics Facts involving numbers or data

STEM An acronym for science, technology, engineering, and math. STEM teaching encourages discovery, creativity, curiosity, and critical thinking.

study (noun) A project in which a group of people research and examine an issue, and report on what they have found

taxes Money that must be paid to the government out of income

time management Dividing one's time between different tasks, and making sure they are completed on schedule

UNESCO Short for United Nations Educational, Scientific and Cultural Organization, a United Nations branch that focuses on international programs that support education, science, and cultural preservation

United Nations An organization to which 193 countries belong, with the aims of international peace and progress

valid Based on facts and proven with evidence

vocational Describes education that is needed for a particular job

volunteer Work that is done for free

LEARNING MORE

Find out more about the arguments concerning education.

Books

Everett, Reese. *Homework, Yes or No*. Rourke Educational Media, 2016.

Everett, Reese. *Smartphones in Class, Yes or No*. Rourke Educational Media, 2016.

Loewen, Nancy. *Writing Powerful Persuasive Pieces*. Lerner Publishing, 2015.

Palmer, Erin. *Summer School, Yes or No*. Rourke Educational Media, 2016.

Websites

Learn more about writing and evaluating arguments and counterclaims:
www.icivics.org/products/drafting-board

This website examines the argument for saving arts education in schools. Read the article, watch the videos, and follow the links to evaluate whether you believe the argument is valid:
https://lawstreetmedia.com/issues/education/cutting-art-programs-schools-solution-part-problem

Read about the benefits and negative effects of using cell phones in school:
www.safesearchkids.com/cell-phones-in-school/#.W0ODcy0ZNBx

Watch this news video from CBS News about an 11-year-old boy who started a debate about homework at his school. Do you agree with his argument?
https://safeshare.tv/x/HFp9Ll11vSg

INDEX

ABOUT THE AUTHOR

James Bow is the author of more than 50 nonfiction books for children. He is a freelance writer and editor who lives with his wife and two daughters.